LIBRARY OF AWESOME ANIMALS

POISON DART FROG

By Jenna Grodzicki

Bearport Publishing

Minneapolis, Minnesota

Credits: Cover and title page, © Studio-Annika/iStock; 3, © Dirk Ercken/Shutterstock; 4, © F. Rauschenbach/F1online digitale Bildagentur GmbH/Alamy; 4–5, © kikkerdirk/iStock; 6L, © Morley Read/Alamy; 6R, © GlobalP/iStock; 7, © Adam Jones/DanitaDelimont/Alamy; 9, © Charles Bergman/Shutterstock; 10–11, © Klaus Ulrich Müller/Alamy; 13, © Thorsten Spoerlein/iStock; 14, © Matthijs Kuijpers/Dreamstime; 15, © Val_th/Dreamstime; 16–17, © Pete Oxford/Minden Pictures; 18–19, © Dirk Ercken/Shutterstock; 20, © Thomas Marent/Minden Pictures; 21, © Jim Zuckerman/Getty Images; 22, © archivector/Shutterstock; and 23, © kikkerdirk/iStock.

Bearport Publishing Company Product Development Team
President: Jen Jenson; Director of Product Development: Spencer Brinker; Senior Editor: Allison Juda; Editor: Charly Haley; Associate Editor: Naomi Reich; Senior Designer: Colin O'Dea; Associate Designer: Elena Klinkner; Product Development Assistant: Anita Stasson

Library of Congress Cataloging-in-Publication Data

Names: Grodzicki, Jenna, 1979- author.
Title: Poison dart frog / by Jenna Grodzicki.
Description: Minneapolis, Minnesota : Bearport Publishing Company, [2023] | Series: Library of awesome animals | Includes bibliographical references and index.
Identifiers: LCCN 2022011022 (print) | LCCN 2022011023 (ebook) | ISBN 9798885091121 (library binding) | ISBN 9798885091190 (paperback) | ISBN 9798885091268 (ebook)
Subjects: LCSH: Dendrobatidae--Juvenile literature.
Classification: LCC QL668.E233 G76 2023 (print) | LCC QL668.E233 (ebook) | DDC 597.8/77--dc23/eng/20220315
LC record available at https://lccn.loc.gov/2022011022
LC ebook record available at https://lccn.loc.gov/2022011023

Copyright © 2023 Bearport Publishing Company. All rights reserved. No part of this publication may be reproduced in whole or in part, stored in any retrieval system, or transmitted in any form or by any means, electronic, mechanical, photocopying, recording, or otherwise, without written permission from the publisher.

For more information, write to Bearport Publishing, 5357 Penn Avenue South, Minneapolis, MN 55419. Printed in the United States of America.

Contents

Awesome Poison Dart Frogs!........... 4
Small but Flashy 6
Armies in the Rain Forest 8
You Are What You Eat 10
Back Off!............................12
Staying Alive 14
Protect the Eggs! 16
Piggyback Ride...................... 18
Growing and Changing 20

Information Station 22
Glossary 23
Index 24
Read More 24
Learn More Online................................. 24
About the Author.................................. 24

AWESOME Poison Dart Frogs!

SLURP! A poison dart frog grabs an insect with its long, sticky tongue. Hopping over leaves or slurping up bugs, poison dart frogs are awesome!

POISON DART FROGS HAVE SUCTION CUPS ON THEIR FEET THAT HELP THEM STICK TO ALMOST ANY SURFACE.

Small but Flashy

Poison dart frogs are teeny tiny, but being small doesn't mean these frogs are hard to see. Their bright colors make them impossible to miss! Poison dart frogs come in almost every color of the rainbow. They can be red, orange, yellow, green, blue, or black. The frogs can have bright patterns with spots or stripes.

Armies in the Rain Forest

These brightly colored frogs live in the **rain forests** of Central America and South America. They hop around in pairs or small groups called armies. From a distance, the frogs blend in with the colorful plants around them. Most stay on the forest floor, where they can hide among leaves and fallen flowers.

POISON DART FROGS COMMUNICATE WITH ONE ANOTHER BY CHIRPING, BUZZING, OR EVEN SCREAMING.

You Are What You Eat

The forest floor holds all the food these frogs need. Ants, fruit flies, termites, crickets, and beetles are on the menu. **YUM!**

But some insects are more than just a tasty meal. Scientists believe the frogs' food helps them become deadly. After they chow down on poisonous insects, the frogs let out that poison through their skin.

ADULT POISON DART FROGS CAN GO FOR DAYS WITHOUT EATING.

Back Off!

The golden poison frog wins the prize for world's most poisonous frog. In fact, it's one of the most poisonous animals on Earth! The Emberá people of Colombia have even used this frog's poison for hunting. They've rubbed the tips of blowgun darts on the frogs' backs and then used the poisoned darts to take down other animals.

Staying Alive

While most **predators** stay away from poison dart frogs, one animal is not affected by their poison. Fire-bellied snakes can gobble up these frogs without getting sick. **YIKES!**

However, the biggest **threats** to poison dart frogs are from humans. Some people catch the frogs to keep as pets. Others are destroying the rain forest **habitats** where frogs live.

Fire-bellied snake

SOME KINDS OF POISON DART FROGS ARE **ENDANGERED**.

Protect the Eggs!

While adult frogs are usually safe from predators, their eggs are more at risk. After **mating**, the **female** poison dart frog finds a dark, damp spot to lay her eggs. Then, both parent frogs guard the eggs to make sure they don't dry out or get eaten by hungry insects.

MOTHER POISON DART FROGS LAY ANYWHERE FROM 1 TO 40 EGGS AT A TIME.

Piggyback Ride

After a couple of weeks, the eggs hatch. Baby frogs start as **tadpoles** that look nothing like their parents! The wormlike creatures without legs must live in water. They wriggle onto their father's back, and he carries them to water nearby. Then, the father leaves, and the tadpoles are on their own.

WHEN THE FATHER GIVES HIS TADPOLES A PIGGYBACK RIDE IT'S CALLED BACKPACKING.

Growing and Changing

The tadpoles stay in water for several months. Then, their bodies begin to change in a process called **metamorphosis** (*met*-uh-MOR-fuh-sis). The tadpoles grow front and back legs. Their long tails shrink until they're completely gone. The tadpoles have become frogs! They leave the water, and they're ready for life on land.
HOP, HOP, HOP!

Information Station

POISON DART FROGS ARE AWESOME!
LET'S LEARN EVEN MORE ABOUT THEM.

Kind of animal: Poison dart frogs are amphibians. Like all amphibians, they live part of their lives in water and part on land. They hatch from eggs and are **cold-blooded**.

More frogs: There are more than 5,000 types of frogs. They can be found on every continent except Antarctica.

Size: Poison dart frogs are about 0.75 to 1.5 inches (2 to 4 cm) long. That's about the same length as a paper clip.

POISON DART FROGS AROUND THE WORLD

WHERE POISON DART FROGS LIVE